FACE TO FACE WITH
CHEETAHS

by Chris Johns
with Elizabeth Carney

NATIONAL
GEOGRAPHIC
WASHINGTON, D.C.

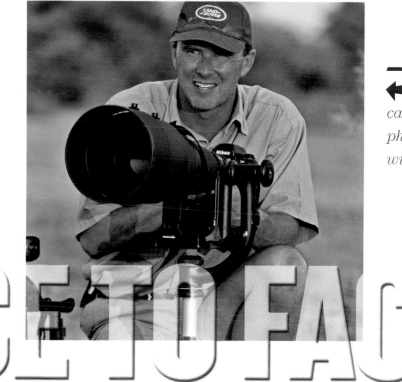

Cheetahs don't smile for the camera, but I do. With my telephoto lens, I can photograph wild animals from far away.

FACE TO FACE

No one is sure why cheetahs have dark "tearstains" running down their cheeks. Experts think the marks may reduce glare from the sun.

Deep in the heart of Africa, I found myself working on the story of my dreams. On assignment for *National Geographic* magazine, I was on the prowl for cheetahs in the Okavango Delta in Botswana. Ever since I became a nature photographer over 20 years ago, I had wanted to photograph these animals. But how could I keep up with a cat that accelerates faster than a race car?

My truck could not match a cheetah's speed, so I knew I had to earn the cats' trust in order to get

CHEETAHS IN HISTORY

■ The ancient Sumerians, who lived in present-day Iraq, were the first to tame cheetahs, around 3000 B.C.

■ In Egypt, royal tombs from about 1650 B.C. show cheetahs wearing collars and leashes. The cats were the prized pets of kings.

■ During the 14th, 15th, and 16th centuries, European princes and nobles hunted with tame cheetahs.

■ The emperor Akbar the Great, who ruled India from 1556 to 1605, is believed to have owned 9,000 hunting cheetahs.

close. In wildlife photography, you always hope for the animals to come to you. One day, a cheetah did just that. We had a face-to-face encounter I will never forget.

For four months, my guide Dave Hamman and I had been following a mother cheetah and her five cubs around the Moremi Game Reserve. We kept a safe distance but paid close attention to the family's habits. For example, we knew where the mother hunted and where she took her cubs to nap and play.

Early one morning, we were watching them. It was a crisp, cloudless day. Kneeling on the ground next to the truck, I snapped pictures of the cubs as they played under their mother's watchful eye. Normally, wild cheetahs keep their distance from humans. They have a natural fear of us. But that morning curiosity got the best of the cats.

One of the cubs came over. First she chewed on a piece of my camera equipment. Then she gnawed on the heel of my boot. My heart pounded with excitement, but I sat perfectly still. Coming closer, she hissed at my hand and then licked it. Her scratchy tongue felt like sandpaper. How amazing to share a moment with such a beautiful wild animal!

The family came close to us on their own terms. We didn't have to lure them. They began to relax and became almost as interested in us as we were in them! But I didn't want the cheetahs to get too comfortable with us and lose their fear of humans completely. That would be dangerous for them, since humans are one of the cheetah's main threats.

With that experience came a lot of responsibility on my part. I knew I had to take the best photographs I could for the magazine article. I wanted the world to know about these amazing animals—and to know that we're in danger of losing them forever.

↑ A cheetah cub practices a surprise attack on his brother. Through this type of play, cheetahs develop survival skills they'll need to make it on their own in the wild. Behaviors like sprinting, tripping, and neck biting are the same things adult cheetahs will do to take down an impala.

MEET

THE CHEETAH

Nature photographers on the African savanna have a lot to worry about. One night, I got a rude awakening when an elephant bumped the truck I slept in. Another day a troop of baboons broke into my guide's tent and ripped up his belongings. And keeping a lookout for dangerous predators like lions and leopards is a must.

In that way, photographers have a lot in common with cheetahs. Cheetahs are forever scanning their surroundings for their next meal and, more

Cheetahs used to live across Africa and parts of Asia, but their range is much more limited today. There are also fewer of them. Only about 10,000 cheetah remain in the wild.

important, for enemies. Lions and other predators will kill cheetah cubs and sometimes adults.

Fortunately, cheetahs are the fastest land animals on the planet. On the open plains, there's nothing they can't outrun. But they're not as strong as other predators. Lions, hyenas, and wild dogs can overpower them, so cheetahs usually try to avoid a fight.

Cheetahs are intelligent and selective hunters. They usually prey on small- to medium-size animals, like gazelles and impalas, and avoid large ones, like zebras and wildebeests. By hunting smaller animals, they are less likely to get hurt. Imagine getting kicked by a 450-pound (205 kg) wildebeest—ouch!

These crafty cats can also be full of surprises. Cheetah researchers were startled by an unusual hunt I recorded. Two cheetah brothers came upon a large antelope called a lechwe. The 250-pound (110 kg) lechwe was larger than cheetahs' usual prey. It ran into a pond, hoping to lose the pair in the water. Instead the brothers teamed up to hold the lechwe's head under water until it drowned.

⬇ Two brother cheetahs work together to drown a lechwe in a small pond. After I photographed this surprising behavior, researchers spotted other cats drowning their prey.

HOW TO CHIRP LIKE A CHEETAH

Unlike great cats such as lions and tigers, cheetahs cannot roar. They do make many other sounds, some of which are unique among cats.

— **Yip:** A high-pitched barking sound cheetahs use to call to one another.

— **Chirp:** A cub's version of a yip, it sounds like the call of a bird.

— **Churr:** A stuttered bark. Cheetahs use this sound in social situations.

— **Growls and hisses:** Used to express annoyance or fear.

This behavior had never been documented before.

Males, usually brothers, often live in groups of two or three, called coalitions. As a group, they have more success at hunting and defending a territory. Female cheetahs, on the other hand, are loners.

Females can cover a range as large as New York City. They do not defend a territory, but they will protect their cubs. In defense of her family, I've seen

a mother cheetah take on two male cheetahs who wanted the family out of their territory. She escaped with only a cut on her leg and her cubs unharmed.

Cubs stay with their mothers until they are about a year and a half old. During this time, their moms protect, feed, and teach them to hunt. Mothers even catch live prey and release it unharmed so that their cubs can practice hunting.

⬆ *This cub is a rare type of cheetah known as a king cheetah. They have darker, longer spots, which run together to form stripes down their backs. Even though they look a little different from other cheetahs, they are members of the same species.*

All this comes at a cost. The large nasal passages mean there's less space for other facial features. As a result, cheetahs have smaller jaws and teeth.

Cheetahs also have to pick the right moment to hunt. Because cheetahs don't defend their prey against other top predators, animals such as lions and hyenas often steal their kills. A mother cheetah does not want to use important stores of energy to kill an antelope, only to have it taken away by a lion.🐾

A cheetah leaps into a tree (left) and another climbs a tall termite mound (right) to search their surroundings for predators and prey. Cheetahs are clumsy climbers because their paws lack the sharp, retractable claws of other species of cats.

RACING

"I'm the only mother he's known," says Laurie Marker of Chewbaaka. Without the skills passed on by their real mothers, captive cubs would not survive if released into the wild.

FOR SURVIVAL

Orphaned as a cub, this cheetah, named Chewbaaka, was rescued by Laurie Marker, the founder of the Cheetah Conservation Fund in Namibia. Chewbaaka lives in captivity and chases mechanical bait for exercise.

After eight months of photographing cheetahs, I was getting ready to head home. On my journey back, I was asked to give a talk about cheetahs at a small museum in Francistown, Botswana. After I finished speaking, one of the first questions was from an eleven-year-old girl. She asked, "What can *I* do to save cheetahs?" *(You can find out how to help on page 26.)*

Many Africans, and people all over the world, are worried about cheetahs' future. Cheetahs are

WITH FRIENDS LIKE THESE ...

Cheetahs don't have many friends on the African savanna. They are constantly on the lookout for danger. Here are some of the cheetahs' worst enemies:

- Lions

- Hyenas

- Leopards

- Human hunters and poachers

Africa's most endangered cat. In the early 1900s, more than 100,000 cheetahs roamed throughout Africa and Asia. Now about 10,000 remain in the wild. Their numbers are greatest in southern Africa, especially Namibia and Botswana. They are nearly extinct in Asia, with only about 60–100 left in Iran.

Cheetahs' numbers plunged for many reasons. For the most part, overhunting and habitat loss are to blame. But because of cheetahs' nature, plans to save them are complex. Africa's main method of protecting endangered animals is to create wildlife reserves where hunting is either restricted or not allowed. But unlike other types of African cats, cheetahs don't thrive in most reserves. Large predators there, such as lions, hyenas, and leopards, kill cheetah cubs and take cheetahs' prey.

In some countries, including Namibia, farmers and ranchers own large areas of land. Cheetahs do well in this environment. In fact, Namibia has the highest population of cheetahs of any African country. This is because farmers keep the number of lions and hyenas low to protect their livestock. With little competition for prey (and fewer threats

A cheetah trapped near injured livestock awaits removal by conservationists. This one was lucky. Trapped cheetahs are often shot.

Talk about a hands-on lesson! At a Namibian school, children pet a tame cheetah that a conservationist brought to teach them about the cats.

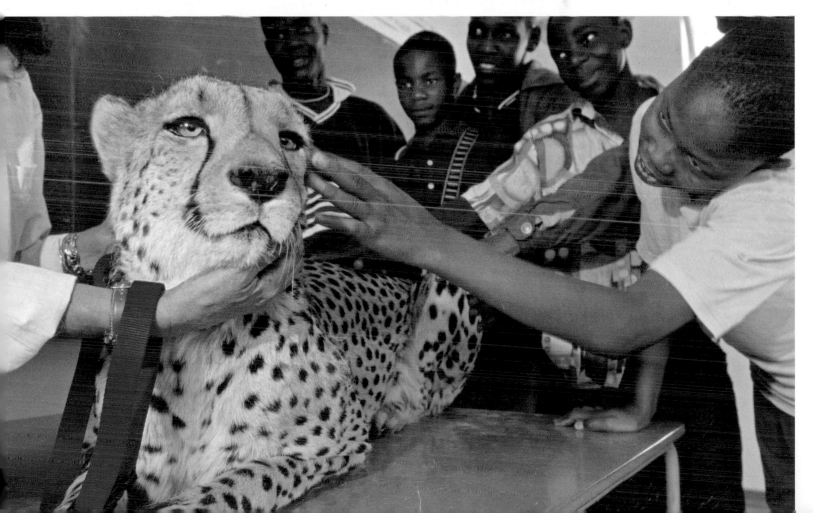

to their cubs), cheetahs have an advantage in these areas. However, like other predators, cheetahs sometimes hunt livestock. That's why African ranchers often trap and shoot cheetahs.

Several organizations are working to help humans and cheetahs live together peacefully. One group, the Cheetah Conservation Fund, has started education programs to teach farmers how to manage and protect livestock without killing cheetahs. Now, farmers sometimes call the group for help when they are having problems with cheetahs, instead of killing them. The group also started a successful program to train dogs called Anatolian shepherds to guard livestock against cheetahs.

Because of efforts like these and the passion of people all over the world who want to save cheetahs, I have hope that these animals can be saved. 🐾

HOW YOU CAN HELP

▼ *These young cheetahs are busy playing, unaware that they are developing the skills they need to survive.*

Africa is a large continent with 53 countries. It has many cities and towns. It is a land of great beauty, with beaches, mountains, forests, grasslands, and deserts.

In some parts of Africa, people are poor, hungry, and suffering from disease. Wars in countries such as Sudan, Rwanda, and the Democratic Republic of the Congo have killed millions of people. Faced with such hardships, it can be difficult to start and maintain animal conservation efforts. People there must use all their resources just to survive. For this reason, saving Africa's people in troubled regions is an important step toward saving the continent's wildlife. People need food, clean water, and access to good health care. Improving the quality of Africans' lives will boost efforts to save the cheetah.

There are many signs of hope in Africa. About 25 million visitors come to the continent each year. Many countries, such as Botswana, are peaceful and have stable governments and conservation policies. Here are some ways you can make a difference in the lives of Africa's people and its animals.

■ The best way for you to help cheetahs is to encourage your family and friends to visit Africa, if possible. This brings money to the economies of African nations.

■ Give or encourage your family to give to charities that fight poverty in Africa.

■ Raise money for conservation organizations such as the Cheetah Conservation Fund, Wildlife Conservation Society, Conservation International, and AfriCat.

■ Learn all you can about cheetahs. Go to zoos that have cheetahs. Study them in school and when you grow up. The more we know about cheetahs, the better we will be able to help them survive.

■ Zoos are not just nice places to see cheetahs, but places where cheetah conservation is actually happening. The National Zoo in Washington, D.C., has a breeding program for cheetahs. You can make donations to the program. Visit http://nationalzoo.si.edu/Animals/AfricanSavanna/CheetahFund/default.cfm.

IT'S YOUR TURN

YOU'RE THE EDITOR!

I'm a photographer, but I'm also the Editor in Chief of *National Geographic* magazine, so reporters, photographers, and researchers look to me for guidance about what stories to cover and how to cover them. Now that you know all about cheetahs, it's your turn to be the Editor in Chief. Pretend you want to run a cover story about cheetahs in an upcoming issue of *National Geographic*. For a cover story, a photograph or picture related to the story is featured on the cover of the magazine. Write instructions for your staff about how you want the story to be written and photographed. Use the following tips as a guide.

WHAT'S THE ANGLE?

An angle is the part of a story that you want to tell. Topics you might choose are saving the cheetah, cheetah hunting behavior, or cheetah family life.

WHAT'S THE ARTICLE ABOUT?

Once you have an angle, write out the questions you want your reporter to explore. If the story is about family life, you might ask: How many cubs do cheetahs have? How do mothers care for their young ones? Think of other questions you could ask.

HOW TO TELL THE STORY IN PICTURES

Tell your photographer what kind of pictures you would like to run with the article. Describe what kind of shots you want and where you think he or she should go to get those pictures.

⬇ *Tourist vehicles are a welcome sight for cheetahs. Guides offer cheetahs snacks of meat to lure them closer to the sightseers.*

FACTS AT A GLANCE

A close-up of a cheetah's spotted fur. Another African cat, the leopard, also has spotted fur. But leopards' spots look very different. They form flower-like patterns, called rosettes. They are black on the outside and tan inside. Cheetahs have solid round or oval spots.

Scientific Name

Scientists use the name *Acinonyx jubatus* for the cheetah. Cheetahs are grouped with other big cats in the family Felidae. All cats belong to a group of animals called Carnivora, which also includes bears, seals, and other predators.

Size

Cheetahs stand about 27–35 inches (68–89 cm) tall and weigh 70–140 pounds (31–63 kg). Compare that to a lion, which can weigh up to 425 pounds (192 kg), and you can see why cheetahs run instead of fighting when a lion shows up!

Life Span

More than 80 percent of cheetah cubs don't survive to adulthood. Some are killed by other predators while the mother cheetah is away hunting, and others die of diseases. The ones that do survive live only four to six years in the wild. Cheetahs in captivity can live to be 15 years old.

Special Features

Cheetahs are very smart hunters. They may be fast, but they can keep up a burst of speed for only about a minute. So they have to plan their hunts very carefully, and sneak up as close to their prey as possible before they attack. One unusual feature of cheetahs is that they pace. Like giraffes and a few other animals, they walk by moving both legs on one side of their body forward, then both legs on the other side.

Habitat and Range

Cheetahs live mainly in southern Africa (Namibia and Botswana) and East Africa (Kenya and Tanzania), in the savanna and semi-desert. About 95 percent of the cheetahs in Namibia live on farmland. In Iran, they live in the mountains.

Diet

Their favorite prey is the Thomson's gazelle, but they also hunt rabbits, birds, and a variety of antelopes. They hunt by tripping their prey and then strangling it with a bite to the neck. Unlike many other big cats, cheetahs hunt during the day.

Reproduction

Except for coalitions and females with cubs, cheetahs are solitary animals. They come together only to mate, and the female raises the cubs by herself. After a 90-day pregnancy, she gives

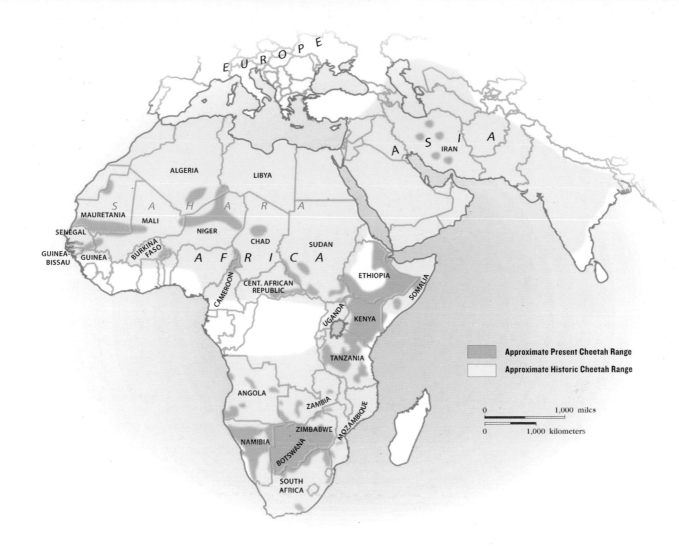

Approximate Present Cheetah Range

Approximate Historic Cheetah Range

birth to three to five cubs in a thicket or rocky area where the babies will be hidden. As they grow, she teaches them to hunt by bringing them live prey to chase. They stay with her for a year or two.

Biggest Threats

Only about 10,000 adult cheetahs are left in the wild. They are considered vulnerable, meaning they have a risk of becoming extinct in the wild. They need large territories to find enough food. As more land is turned into farmland, less land is left for cheetahs and other wildlife. They also compete with other predators. Humans sometimes kill them to protect livestock. Also, all cheetahs are very closely related to one another. As a result, their immune systems are not strong and they are at risk for many diseases.

This map shows cheetahs' range as it was around the year 1900, when cheetahs could be found throughout Africa and Asia. Today, they live mostly in southern and East Africa, with a small population in Iran.

GLOSSARY

Coalition: A group of two or three male cheetahs, often brothers, who live and hunt together.

Endangered: Describes a species that has very few individuals remaining. If the number of individuals rises, the species classification may change to "threatened" or "recovered." If the number falls, the species may become "extinct," meaning no individuals are left.

Habitat: The local environment in which an animal lives.

Impala: A type of antelope.

Mammals: Air-breathing, warm-blooded animals with hair whose offspring nurse on their mother's milk.

Mantle: A soft, fluffy mane of hair on the back of cubs' necks. It may help disguise them when they hide.

Predator: An animal that must kill other animals for food.

Prey: Animals that predators—like cheetahs—eat. Gazelles and rabbits are examples of prey.

Savanna: Grasslands in Africa that are home to elephants, lions, giraffes, and many other animals.

Species: A group of animals or plants that look similar and can breed with one another, and whose offspring also can breed successfully.

Territory: The area in which an animal lives. Cheetahs need a territory of several hundred square miles in order to have enough prey to hunt.

FIND OUT MORE

Books & Articles

Eaton, Randall L. *The Cheetah: Nature's Fastest Racer.* New York: Dodd, Mead, 1981.

Hansen, Rosanna. *Caring for Cheetahs: My African Adventure.* Honesdale, PA: Boyds Mills Press, 2007.

Hopcraft, Xan, and Carol Cawthra Hopcraft. *How It Was with Dooms: A True Story from Africa.* New York: Margaret K. McElderry Books (Simon & Schuster Children's Publishing Division), 1997.

Hunter, Luke, and Dave Hamman. *Cheetah.* Cape Town, South Africa: Struik Publishers, 2003.

Movies

Duma (2005). http://dumamovie.warner bros.com. A boy journeys across Africa to return his best friend, a cheetah named Duma, to the wild.

Web Sites

The National Zoo is breeding cheetahs. See http://nationalzoo.si.edu/Animals/African Savanna/fact-cheetah.cfm.

The Cheetah Conservation Fund Web site is at http://www.cheetah.org.

Information about cheetahs and sound files of cheetahs chirping and purring are available at http://africaguide.com/wildlife/cheetah.htm.

National Geographic Animal pages at http://animals.nationalgeographic.com/animals/mammals/cheetah.html?nav=A-Z have fact sheets and videos about cheetahs. You can also use the search engine to find pictures and information about other African animals mentioned here, such as the Thomson's gazelle, wildebeests, lechwes, and baboons.

INDEX

RESEARCH & PHOTOGRAPHIC NOTES

The gallery in the Botswana museum was packed with people who had come to see the photographs I've taken of cheetahs in the Okavango Delta. A lecture followed. Afterward, a girl with sparkling brown eyes shyly raised her hand. "What can *I* do to save cheetahs?" she asked.

I broke the silence to tell a story about two cheetahs I'd photographed. I call them the Steroid Boys, because of their impressive muscles. They were hungry and spotted a herd of red lechwe, powerful antelopes that graze in flooded areas. The Boys rushed the herd and separated a large male who ran into deep water. Water splashed as one cheetah jumped on the antelope's back, while the other climbed on his head, between its large, sharp horns. The weight of the cat pushed his prey's head under water. The antelope drowned.

My camera had captured cheetah behavior that baffled biologists. When they saw the photographs, they were surprised. The drowning was an accident, they said; cheetahs don't drown their prey—they choke it. But this was no accident. Over the next few months several groups on safari saw the Steroid Boys drown antelope again. The experts were wrong.

I told the young girl that she can help save cheetahs by becoming a wildlife biologist. There is so much we don't know about cheetahs. We need scientists dedicated to studying them so we can make better decisions to ensure their survival. Time is running out. Cheetah populations are shrinking fast.

Share your passion for the world's fastest land animal and help people realize the value of wild places. Encourage family and friends to visit the bush. No dream is too big. Become a game guide. Run your own safari camp. Reach a wider audience by becoming a photographer, writer, or filmmaker. Or become a teacher. Share with your students the wonder and diversity of nature. Solutions come to those who are informed and inspired. Whichever path you take, stay close to nature. Learn about it. Appreciate it. Enjoy it. It will enrich your life.   —CJ

The publisher gratefully acknowledges the assistance of Christine Kiel, K–3 curriculum and reading consultant, and Dr. Laurie Marker, Co-Founder and Executive Director of the Cheetah Conservation Fund, for her assistance with the maps.

Book design by David M. Seager. The body text of the book is set in ITC Century. The display text is set in Knockout and Party Noid.

Front cover: Face to face with the speedy cheetah
Front flap: A young cheetah smiles for the camera.
Back cover: Chris Johns makes a new friend.
Title page: A cheetah bounds into the book.

Published by the National Geographic Society

John M. Fahey, Jr., *President and Chief Executive Officer*

Gilbert M. Grosvenor, *Chairman of the Board*

Tim T. Kelly, *President, Global Media Group*

Nina D. Hoffman, *Executive Vice President; President, Book Publishing Group*

Staff for This Book

Nancy Laties Feresten, *Vice President, Editor-in-Chief of Children's Books*

Bea Jackson, *Design and Illustrations Director, Children's Books*

Jennifer Emmett, Mary Beth Oelkers-Keegan, *Project Editors*

David M. Seager, *Art Director*

Lori Epstein, *Illustrations Editor*

Jocelyn G. Lindsay, *Researcher*

Jean Cantu, *Illustrations Specialist*

Carl Mehler, *Director of Maps*

Rebecca Baines, *Editorial Assistant*

Jennifer A. Thornton, *Managing Editor*

R. Gary Colbert, *Production Director*

Lewis R. Bassford, *Production Manager*

Maryclare Tracy, Nicole Elliott, *Manufacturing Managers*

Susan Borke, *Legal and Business Affairs*

Library of Congress Cataloging-in-Publication Data

Johns, Chris.
Face to face with cheetahs / by Chris Johns with Elizabeth Carney.
    p. cm.
 ISBN 978-1-4263-0323-4 (trade)—ISBN 978-1-4263-0324-1 (library)
1. Cheetah—Africa. 2. Cheetah—Africa—Pictorial works. I. Carney, Elizabeth, 1981- II. Title.
QL737.C23J58 2008
599.75'9--dc22

2007041220

Founded in 1888, the National Geographic Society is one of the largest nonprofit scientific and educational organizations in the world. It reaches more than 285 million people worldwide each month through its official journal, NATIONAL GEOGRAPHIC, and its four other magazines; the National Geographic Channel; television documentaries; radio programs; films; books; videos and DVDs; maps; and interactive media. National Geographic has funded more than 8,000 scientific research projects and supports an education program combating geographic illiteracy.

For more information, please call 1-800-NGS LINE (647-5463) or write to the following address:

National Geographic Society
1145 17th Street N.W.
Washington, D.C. 20036-4688 U.S.A.

Visit us online at
www.nationalgeographic.com/books

For information about special discounts for bulk purchases, please contact National Geographic Books Special Sales: ngspecsales@ngs.org

For rights or permissions inquiries, please contact National Geographic Books Subsidiary Rights: ngbookrights@ngs.org.

Printed in China